Straight Talk!
About Estate Planning

The Truth About Leaving
A Legacy of Love, Wisdom and Wealth

By

Peggy R. Hoyt, J.D., M.B.A.
Deborah E. Roser, J.D.

Dedication

This book is dedicated to our loving fathers,
who wait for us in Heaven.

Peggy's father, John A. Hoyt
Debbie's father, George A. Muntwyler

We are blessed to still enjoy the company and
friendship of our loving mothers,

Gertrude "Trudy" Hoyt and Evelyn Muntwyler

Straight Talk!
About Estate Planning

The Truth About Leaving
A Legacy of Love, Wisdom and Wealth

ISBN 978-0-9823220-2-4

Published by Gratitude Partners, LLC
Chuluota, FL 32766
Phone (407) 977-8080
Fax (407) 977-8078

Cover Design by Pete Mancinelli
www.freelance11.com

TABLE OF CONTENTS

CHAPTER ONE
WHEN I WIN THE LOTTERY, IF I DIE – WHY DO ESTATE PLANNING?

Nothing is so fatiguing as the eternal hanging on
of an uncompleted task.
~William James

Americans are optimistic. We talk about *"When* I win the lottery, and *if* I die." In a perfect world, those would be lofty goals. The reality is few of us will ever win significant amounts of money and nobody is going to get out of here alive. Why is it then we are hesitant to think about, talk about and plan for those events in our lives that are inevitable and have real potential for creating unnecessary grief and expense for our family?

Who has an estate plan? Everyone! That's because if you don't create your own estate plan, your home state is happy to create one for you. Sadly, it is rarely the plan you would create for yourself if you had the education and tools necessary to make well-informed decisions. We applaud you for taking the time to read this book. It means you have enough interest in this topic to become educated about what you can do and accomplish for the protection of yourself and your loved ones.

You might be surprised to learn that most estate plans don't work. If you've ever heard someone say about a loved one who passed away, "Boy if they only knew what was going on, they would be rolling over in their grave!" – that's a classic example of an estate plan that didn't work. Something went wrong. What that something was could be a myriad of things – maybe an unwanted probate, unexpected taxes, unintended beneficiaries, unequal distributions, business succession issues, family hostility, and the list goes on.

A primary goal of estate planning should be to create a plan that works – for you and for your family. No two families are alike and as a result, no two plans will ever be alike. Estate planning is not for the faint of heart and should never be left to a form found online – there are too many unexpected and potentially devastating consequences. Contrary to public sentiment, there is no boilerplate "one size fits all" when it comes to estate planning.

If you were asked to prepare your neighbor's estate plan or your co-worker's estate plan, could you? Chances are you wouldn't even know where to start without asking some pointed questions. Relevant issues include whether the person is married, single or in an unmarried relationship; and if there are minor children, a special needs child, or if there are adult children with an addiction or in a bad marriage. Does this person have children from another marriage or a family business? Do you know how their assets are titled, how their beneficiaries are named or if there are any estate tax issues? These questions are just the tip of the iceberg.

Estate planning implicates many other areas of the law. Areas of legal impact can include family law, real estate law, banking law, homestead law, guardianship law, probate and trust administration law, tax law and contract law, to name a few. Unless you're an expert in each of these areas of the law and know how they affect your family, there is a better than even probability that significant mistakes will be made if you attempt to plan without a professional.

You will come across many well-meaning individuals and professionals in your day-to-day activities. You'll find them in the form of realtors, bankers, financial advisors, insurance agents, title agents and car sales personnel, to name a few – almost anyone can be in a position to give advice that may have an impact on your estate planning and your ultimate family protection goals. For example, when you open a bank account, you will probably be asked for ownership instructions or a beneficiary designation. How you title your account and who you name as beneficiary may conflict with your overall plan.

Debbie was preparing a financial power of attorney for a friend's father. The father's bank told the friend she should just put her name on her father's bank account. However, that would not have allowed her to help her father with investments, government benefits, taxes, and all the other things typically addressed in a general and comprehensive power of attorney. Rarely do any of these well-meaning people have all the information they need to provide you with a comprehensive plan that will allow your plan to work. Only when all your professionals work together, with your goals in mind, can you have true confidence the plan you're creating will work the way you intend.

Remember, it's your family, your loved ones, and your wishes and goals. Work with a qualified legal professional who has expertise and experience in estate planning and elder law – and someone who will listen, answer your questions and help you understand how your plan will work. Only then can you have certainty your plan has the greatest probability of success. Anything less will result in a plan that only represents wishful thinking and likely will not be a plan at all.

CHAPTER TWO
YOUR HEALTH IN TRUSTED HANDS

Health is like money, we never have a true idea
of its value until we lose it.
~Josh Billings

Unlocking Protected Health Information

"I don't have anything." This is often what we hear when we begin talking about "estate planning." The truth is most people have more than they think. You have loved ones, and you will want to decide who will receive what. Many people believe an "estate plan" is having a will, but it's more comprehensive. We'll save the discussion about wills for a later chapter. However, one of the first questions we ask our clients is "Who will talk to your doctors and make health care decisions for you if you can't make them for yourself?"

Debbie sometimes starts her workshops with the statement, "I'm never going to get sick." For some reason, nobody believes her! Some of us do get through life with minimal illness and only a few accidents. Most of us do get sick from time to time, and have had at least one surgery and maybe an accident or two. If it hasn't happened to you, you probably know someone who has been sick or has been involved in a car accident. As we write this, Debbie's mother was released from the hospital, one friend just had three surgeries for the same problem, and another friend was diagnosed with cancer and is facing seven weeks of chemotherapy and radiation.

So what happens if tomorrow you are on your way home from work or shopping and all of a sudden you are struck from behind by someone in a much bigger hurry than you? Your car starts spinning, finally coming to rest in the median after hitting two more cars. You hit your head on the steering wheel, and you are now unconscious. This is just one possible scenario, and while we know it always happens to "the other guy," what *can* happen is limited only by your imagination.

Everyone runs the risk of an accident resulting in a temporary state of unconsciousness or, worse yet, brain injury or coma. Every night on the news we hear about someone who was involved in a car accident, was the victim of a violent crime, had a motorcycle accident, experienced a slip and fall at home or work, had a heart attack or stroke, or had a skiing accident. Recently, Debbie read about a woman whose car went off the road and got stuck in a ditch. She got out of the car, walked to the side of the road and was struck and killed. Unfortunately, the list of possibilities is endless, as are the potential devastating health effects. If you cannot imagine what *could* happen, think about what *has* happened to your own family members and friends. Can it happen to you?

A multitude of issues arise for the EMT's and first responders to an accident. These issues continue for emergency room doctors and other health care providers as you arrive at the hospital. The first issue is who has the authority to give doctors health information when you get to the hospital?

In 1996, Congress enacted the Health Insurance Portability and Accountability Act (HIPAA). Several years later came The Privacy Rule, created to assure an individual's health information is properly protected while allowing the flow of health information needed to provide and promote high quality health care. With limited exceptions, a health care provider may not disclose protected health information without a patient's express written authorization. Failure to follow these rules is a criminal offense and can also result in heavy monetary penalties. After all, would you want your doctor telling your neighbor about your health condition?

If you are in the hospital in Buffalo, New York, and someone you know (your sister, daughter, father or cousin) from Myrtle Beach, South Carolina, calls the hospital to find out about your condition, what is the result?   If you are not capable of speaking to them because you are unconscious, and there is nothing in writing from you giving any of them permission to receive information about your health condition, they likely won't be getting any information. They will be left in the dark, not knowing who to turn to or what to do.

A few months ago, just days after completing an estate plan for a client, Debbie's client went by ambulance to the hospital for a possible heart attack. Her daughter called the hospital to get a report on her mother. However, without authorization, the nurses were unwilling to provide that daughter with any information about her mother or her condition. The first step is providing certain loved ones access to your health information and your health care providers through a HIPAA authorization.

De-Stressing Your Doctors

The ambulance has made it safely to the hospital and you are taken by stretcher to the emergency room, where a doctor is there to meet you. You don't know it, because you are unconscious. Your doctor is given the history of the accident. Do you think your doctor would like to talk with someone about your condition, about medications you may be taking, and about health conditions from which you may suffer? Aside from who can *speak* to your doctor, who will actually make health care *decisions* for you? For example, if your doctor needs to order x-rays and tests, who will authorize them? What if you need surgery or certain medications? Unless you have specified in writing the individual who will be your health care surrogate, your doctors will be at a loss as to who to talk to and who can make decisions for you.

Some states have special laws that dictate who will be your health care surrogate if you fail to choose one. If your state does have such a law, do you know who your state has chosen for you? We believe that regardless of who the state has chosen for you, it is always best if *you* make the decision about who will speak for you should circumstances ever require it. Otherwise, the results could be disastrous.

For example, if your state has chosen your spouse to make your health care decisions if you can't, and you are in the process of getting a divorce, he or she would probably not be your first choice. What if the state's choice is an estranged child you have not spoken to in more than 10 years? Or a sibling who lives overseas? Even worse, if you are in an unmarried relationship, your partner will generally be the very last person on the list of authorized persons to make your health care decisions.

In a worst case scenario, it is possible your family will need to subject you to the protection of the guardianship court. This means the local probate judge will determine your capacity, choose a guardian for you and determine what authority that person will have to make your health care decisions. Unfortunately, the person the judge chooses may not be consistent with the person you would have chosen.

Who pays for your guardianship proceeding? You do! It is likely to cost thousands of dollars, considerably more than the average cost of a comprehensive estate plan. We say a guardianship is the worst kind of law suit – it's one your family files against you, you get to pay for it, and ultimately, you lose.

Whether you would choose your husband, your sister, your parent, your partner or your best friend to be your health care surrogate, part of the estate planning process is ensuring you are taken care of as you wish in the event of your incapacity. You'll want to carefully consider who should be a part of your "helper" team to come to your aid when you need them. It starts with naming a person or persons who can speak with your health care providers and it continues with naming a surrogate who can make health care decisions for you if you cannot.

How To Choose Your Voice and Who Should Listen In

When you consider who will make your health care decisions if you can't, choose someone you trust – someone who will make the decisions you would make. This is not an opportunity for your surrogate to make decisions your surrogate would choose. Your surrogate's job is to make decisions he or she believes you would make. For example, if you don't believe in blood transfusions and your surrogate does, you have to be comfortable your surrogate will follow your wishes and ignore his or her own. Some people can make decisions inconsistent with their own beliefs, others would find it difficult, and many would find it impossible. Of course, if your surrogate is unaware of your health care and medical beliefs, such as avoiding a blood transfusion, your surrogate may unwittingly act against your wishes.

As a result, your surrogate must know enough about you to know what you would choose. Your surrogate should know your health conditions and your medications, or have access to that information when needed, and your surrogate should especially know if you have strong feelings about any particular treatment. Your chosen surrogate should also have demonstrated care and concern for your welfare and be able to visit you and meet with your health care providers. Your surrogate should also be aware of your religious and moral beliefs.

As discussed in the previous section, you also want to decide who can speak with your health care professionals. Consider Jeffrey, who is 85 and just had a stroke. His wife of 60 years, Maggie, is distraught and confused. Jeffrey cannot speak for himself and has named Maggie as his health care surrogate. Certainly Maggie knows Jeffrey well and intends to make every decision Jeffrey would wish to make. However, when Maggie listens to Jeffrey's doctor, she feels frightened and confused and is not certain what questions she should ask. Maggie would like to consult with her three children and her grandchildren, many of whom are already at the hospital. However, only Maggie has been authorized to talk with the doctors, so Maggie must go to her children and grandchildren and try to repeat what the doctor has told her. This may not be the ideal situation for Maggie, or for Jeffrey, because Maggie may not recall everything the doctor said.

During Jeffrey's planning process, we would recommend that while Maggie remains the one who ultimately makes Jeffrey's health care decisions, other family members be given permission to speak with Jeffrey's doctors as well. Typically the surrogate, who is close to the ailing person, is under a tremendous amount of anxiety and is probably sleep deprived. Maggie may find it difficult to concentrate as she speaks to Jeffrey's doctors. Some of her anxiety can be alleviated by allowing Jeffrey's doctors to speak with other family members as well. The other family members can then assist the doctors in helping the surrogate understand and assimilate the information necessary to make an informed decision. So Jeffrey, while he is well, may wish to include his children and grandchildren, or a selection of each, to also have permission to also talk with his doctors.

Does Your Family Know Your End-of-Life Decisions?

On February 25, 1990, 26-year-old Terri Schiavo collapsed in her St. Petersburg, Florida, home in full cardiac arrest. She suffered massive brain damage due to lack of oxygen and, after two and a half months in a coma, her diagnosis was elevated to vegetative state. Terri's husband, Michael, pursued efforts to rehabilitate her until 1998. In 1998, Michael petitioned the court for removal of Terri's feeding tube.

Terri had not memorialized her end-of-life wishes in any document. Her parents, Robert and Mary Schindler, disagreed with Michael and wanted Terri maintained on life support. Multiple legal appeals ensued following Michael's request to remove life support. One issue was whether Michael, as Terri's husband, and in the absence of a written direction from Terri, had the right to request termination of life prolonging procedures as a result of Terri's persistent vegetative state.

In 2000, testimony from 18 witnesses was taken regarding Terri's medical condition and her end-of-life wishes. Terri's parents argued that if Terri was conscious, she would not refuse nutrition and hydration, even by artificial means. Michael disagreed and ultimately, Terri's feeding tube was removed. However, the saga continued for several more years.

First, Florida Governor Jeb Bush intervened with a new law called "Terri's Law," and Terri's feeding tube was reinserted. Terri's Law was later overturned and found to be unconstitutional. Would you want your Governor making your end-of-life decisions?

Then, in 2005, the United States Senate attempted to intervene with its own law, and President Bush flew to Washington, D.C. from his vacation in Texas to sign legislation that would keep Terri alive. On that issue, the U.S. Supreme Court declined to grant the Schindlers' further appeals, effectively ending their judicial options. Would you want the President making your end-of-life decisions?

After seven years, 14 appeals and numerous motions, petitions and hearings in front of 19 different Florida state court judges, and involvement by the Florida Governor and the United States President, Terri Schiavo's feeding tube was permanently removed, and she died under hospice care on March 31, 2005. Terri's situation attracted a great deal of public attention, primarily because Terri left no instructions and family members disagreed about her wishes. This case brought to light the importance of having written living will instructions regarding end-of-life decisions.

Regardless of your beliefs regarding the removal or retention of life prolonging procedures, it is imperative you memorialize your wishes in writing. Your living will should also address such things as pain medications or treatments, surgical procedures and the use of a No Code or Do Not Resuscitate order. Every state has different laws regarding end-of-life decisions. A few states have adopted death with dignity provisions allowing individuals the right to choose the time and place of their death. Be sure to consult with an attorney in your state to make sure your health care decisions and your end-of-life wishes are memorialized and are consistent with your state's law.

Health care and end-of-life decisions are an integral part of a comprehensive estate plan designed with your goals in mind. If your estate planning professional is only focused on what happens to your things after you die, you must voice your concerns to ensure you and your family have all the protection needed while you are alive.

CHAPTER THREE
HUMPTY DUMPTY FELL OFF THE WALL –
WHAT HAPPENS IF YOU BECOME MENTALLY DISABLED?

Take care of your body. It's the only place you have to live.
~Jim Rohn

In October 2009, Anthony Marshall, son of Brooke Astor, a socialite and long-reigning matriarch of New York City, was convicted on charges he defrauded his mother and stole tens of millions of dollars from her as she suffered from Alzheimer's in the twilight of her life. A decided and respected philanthropist, Brooke Astor gave away millions of dollars to needy individuals and civic causes in New York City. She died in 2007 at the age of 105. The charges against Anthony arose from a guardianship filed by her grandson, Philip Marshall, who accused his father of looting Mrs. Astor's apartment of art, transferring her properties to his name and keeping her in squalid conditions, confined to a sofa smelling of urine and subsisting on oatmeal and peas.

This story may sound unbelievable and you might imagine it could never happen to you. Unfortunately, it is not only the very wealthy who are exploited. We continue to hear stories of the elderly or infirm who can no longer take care of their own property and finances and are preyed upon by those who pretend to help, but are really just helping themselves to the person's property and money.

Many of us will at some time need someone else to handle our legal and financial affairs, even if only temporarily, as a result of a mental disability. You could be ill and in the hospital, injured from a car accident or a fall from a horse, or be in or in need of long term care and social services as a result of Alzheimer's or dementia.

If you are married, you probably think you can rely on your spouse. In most cases, you can. However, what happens if your spouse dies first or is already ill or is injured in a common accident? Debbie heard about a couple who entered the hospital together and had only named each other as the individual authorized to make property and financial decisions. Luckily, they both recovered and were released from the hospital. Otherwise, there was nobody nominated who could have legally acted on their behalf. Aside from the fact that one never knows what will happen, couples often travel together and can be injured together. For that reason, it is important to name others who can act on your behalf if your spouse is unable.

A first step in creating your estate plan is making sure there is no question or issue about who will make medical, legal and financial decisions for you if your mental capacity is at issue. As we discussed in Chapter Two, your plan should first include a HIPAA medical records authorization permitting loved ones to speak with your doctors, a health care power of attorney (naming your health care surrogate), and a living will regarding your end-of-life wishes. Your health care surrogates and legal agents are both critical in providing protection for you when you are not capable of making decisions for yourself – a condition we sometimes refer to as "alive, but not living." Your legal and health care directives, along with your helpers, can prevent judicial intervention in the form of a guardianship.

Your estate planning strategy should also include a financial durable power of attorney – a document that identifies an agent or attorney-in-fact who will act for you with respect to your finances and property, especially in situations where you cannot act for yourself. Without a financial power of attorney, guardianship is likely in the event of a mental incapacity.

It is important your financial power of attorney is specific, clear and comprehensive. You will want your power of attorney to address not only real and personal property, bank accounts, and investment accounts, but also such things as mail, safe deposit boxes, pets, Medicaid planning techniques, Government benefits, taxes, insurance, retirement accounts and trusts. These are just some of the many powers you should discuss with your attorney. In some states, if a specific power is not set out in the power of attorney, your agent cannot act for you. Florida, for example, has a comprehensive statute on powers of attorney, and a power of attorney that essentially says "my agent can do everything I can do," will not be recognized because it is too general. Specificity is required for a power of attorney to ensure your wishes will be followed.

We ask our clients "If the power is in the document and your agent never has to use that power, do we care?" Most answer "No," because they understand it's what we call "a sweater in the suitcase" – an extra item that's nice to have if we need it, but just extra paper if we don't. We see far too many two to seven page powers of attorney that neglect potentially necessary powers. If your agent needs a power and it is not in your document, your agent will have no choice but to turn to the guardianship court, and then it will be a judge who decides not only who your agent will be but also what actions your agent may take for your benefit. Advance planning gives you the control to make certain your choices and your wishes are known.

It's impossible to guarantee you will never be taken advantage of. However, with proper planning and careful thought as to the persons best suited to provide careful and attentive decision making for you, you can better protect yourself and your loved ones. If you are unmarried or widowed and don't have children you can trust and your choice of friends is limited, decisions related to your agents and surrogates can be challenging. Even when the decision is a difficult one, we still believe it is best for you to make the decision rather than leave the decision to others – unintended family, a professional guardian, or worse, a guardianship judge.

As we mentioned, we view guardianship as the worst type of lawsuit. It is one your family or friends file against you, you get to pay for it and ultimately, you lose. A guardianship is expensive, time consuming, a public process and full of uncertainty. In addition, guardianship court is also generally not where your family wishes to be when you are ill. A well-conceived estate plan will contemplate the possibility of mental disability and plan for the most favorable outcome.

In addition to powers of attorney, living trusts can also provide protection in the event of a mental disability. A living trust will allow you to decide who makes your disability determination, who takes over if you become mentally disabled and what that person can do with respect to the assets owned or controlled by your trust. Peggy has always been an advocate of living trusts for their superior disability planning possibilities. If Peggy falls off her horse, hits her head and needs someone to make her financial decisions, her living trust names those people she trusts and sets out how her money can be spent – not only for her care, but for the support of her spouse and her pets. She would never have the ability to ensure her pets were cared for if a judge held the decision making power.

We can't stress enough how important it is you give careful attention to your choice of agent or successor trustee. A good counseling oriented attorney can help you understand the personal qualities to consider when choosing your agent and successors. Again, nobody can ever guarantee your chosen helpers will never take advantage of you. Debbie used to be a litigator, and people would sometimes ask "What if the witness lies on the stand?" You can't control whether someone chooses to lie, just as you can't control whether someone will choose to steal. This is why the final step is so important.

The final step is keeping your disability plan relevant to your current situation. Even if your power of attorney is well-drafted, if it is more than a few years old or there has been a change in the law or it still identifies your agent daughter by her maiden name, your bank or other financial institution may consider it stale and not honor it. If you have not reviewed your power of attorney recently, you may find it names someone you no longer trust. If that is the case, do not hesitate to see an attorney to revise your power of attorney to name a new agent and successors. You never know when an accident or illness will strike, and the time to find out your plan doesn't work isn't when you need it most.

It's never too early to plan,
but you never know when it will be too late.

CHAPTER FOUR
WHERE THERE'S A WILL, THERE'S A WAY –
OR IS THERE?

If you have built castles in the air, your work need not be lost;
that is where they should be.
Now put the foundations under them.
~Henry David Thoreau

A last will and testament sets forth your wishes regarding distribution of your assets when you die. It also names the person or persons who will be responsible for the administration of your estate – your personal representative or executor. Your will only controls the assets you own in your *individual* name. A will guarantees probate, a process most people believe they would like to avoid.

This chapter could also be titled "Why Plans Don't Work." We want to tell you a story about Mary. Mary is 68 years old, lives is Sarasota, Florida, is a widow and has three children, John, Susan and Robert. John also lives in Sarasota. Susan lives in Minneapolis, Minnesota, and Robert lives in Bradenton, Florida. Mary decides she needs to get her estate plan in order, so she goes to see Harry Hurry, Esquire, for a will. She tells Harry exactly what she wants – a will that leaves her estate as follows:

John is to receive 35%

Susan is to receive 35%

Robert is to receive 30%

Harry prepares the will just as Mary asked and charges a nominal fee of $250.00. Harry never asked Mary about her assets – what she owns, how her assets are titled or how her beneficiaries are designated. Do you think it's important for Harry to talk with Mary about her assets? You might wonder why a lawyer needs to know anything about your assets – is it because if they know what you have, they may charge you more?

Let's take a look at Mary's assets and see if it's important for Harry to know more about them. Mary has the following assets:

Home (with no debt)	$240,000
Money market checking	$45,000
Life insurance (death benefit)	$100,000
Traditional IRA account	$630,000

Mary's assets total $1,015,000 If we look at Mary's will, we know she wants her assets distributed as follows:

John is to receive 35%	$355,250
Susan is to receive 35%	$355,250
Robert is to receive 30%	$304,500

Ok, so far, so good – or is it? Is that the end of the conversation Harry should have with Mary about her assets? To answer that question, let's explore a little further and talk with Mary about how her assets are owned or titled and what her beneficiary designations say.

A few years ago, Mary had a heart attack. She's fine now, but the experience scared her. Like many people who experience a sudden illness or accident, she realized she should put things in order for her family. Like so many others, one of Mary's concerns was that she wanted to avoid probate. She was also concerned that if she became ill again, someone should be in a position to pay her bills and manage her financial affairs.

As soon as Mary felt better after her heart attack, she went to the local office supply store and purchased a quit claim deed form for about $10.00. She put John on the title of her home, because she wanted to avoid probate and she heard if she added John to the title, then her home would pass directly to him on her death and would not have to go through probate. Mary was unaware she may have created several potential problems for herself.

First, Mary just gave up complete control of her home. If Mary ever wants to sell her home for any reason, or if she wants to lease it or mortgage it, she will need John's consent and permission. What if Mary decides she wants to downsize to a condominium and John doesn't think it's a good idea? What if Mary decides she really wants to enjoy her retirement and wants to sell her home and take an around-the-world cruise, but John doesn't like that idea? What if Mary meets the second man of her dreams and decides to sell her home and move to North

Carolina to marry her new love, but John doesn't like that idea either? Mary could be stuck! The cost of avoiding probate may be more than Mary ultimately wants to pay.

Second, Mary's home may now be subject to John's creditors. We haven't started talking with Mary about her family yet, so we don't know what John's credit situation is. However, we do know that bad things happen to good people – a person can lose his or her job, cause an accident, suffer a bankruptcy, or be the victim of a lawsuit for any number of reasons. Mary may have put herself at serious financial risk by adding John's name to her home.

Third, upon making the gift to John, Mary was required to file a gift tax return. Chances are good she didn't even think about this (or maybe she didn't even know she had to). When Mary put John's name on the title to her home, she made a gift to him of $120,000 (one half of the fair market value). Today, an individual can gift up to $13,000 annually to anyone without reporting the gift to the Internal Revenue Service ("IRS") or paying any taxes. This is called the annual gift tax exclusion amount. Gifts in excess of $13,000 annually require the filing of a gift tax return known as a Form 709. No actual tax may be due, but that depends on whether Mary has made other gifts during her lifetime and whether she has used her lifetime gift exclusion (currently $5,120,000 but expected to change to a lower amount on December 31, 2012). Failure to report gifts over $13,000 may subject Mary to an IRS penalty.

Sometimes our clients ask how the IRS will ever discover an unreported gift. The answer falls into the same category as failure to file your annual income tax return. The law requires you to report your income. The law also requires you to report gifts made over the annual exclusion amount. The IRS recognizes that millions of dollars of unreported gifts are made annually and they are taking steps to identify people who are violating the law. Checking the public records for recorded deeds is just one way the IRS is discovering reporting violations. Peggy sometimes tells her clients to ask the person in the cell next to them how the IRS found out about unfiled taxes or unreported gifts.

A fourth potential problem with the addition of John to Mary's house is a capital gains tax concern. When Mary transferred a half interest in her home to John, he took the same tax basis Mary had when she bought the property. If Mary waited and gave John the property upon her death, his tax basis would be increased to the fair market value of the property as of the date of her death. By way of example, if Mary paid $100,000 for her home and she transfers a one half interest to John, his tax basis is $50,000. If the property is sold during Mary's lifetime for its current value of $240,000, Mary has a capital gain of $70,000 and John has a capital gain of $70,000, and both may owe taxes. At the current capital gain tax rate of 15% (and without an exemption), the total tax owed by each will be $21,000. If John had inherited the entire property at Mary's death at a fair market value of $240,000, John would receive a full step up in tax basis and could have sold the property and paid *no* capital gains tax, a savings of $21,000 (or double that if you consider Mary didn't have to pay any capital gains tax either). Do you think John could have used the $21,000 that now has to go to pay taxes? We understand many people want to avoid probate due to the potential cost, the possible delays and its public nature. However, sometimes do it yourself attempts to avoid probate can actually be more costly.

A fifth possible problem with the transfer by Mary to John may be a loss of her homestead ad valorem tax benefits. In many states, homestead property is entitled to preferential tax treatment resulting in both a potential annual property tax savings and a cap on the amount of the annual increase in property taxes. Adding an owner who does not qualify to claim the home as his or her homestead can result in a total or partial loss of this preferential tax treatment. In some cases, it may require the payment of significant back taxes.

Finally, is it possible John is an unintended beneficiary of Mary's home? If we look at Mary's last will, the answer will be a resounding "Yes!" Mary's last will says each child is to receive a specific percentage distribution. If John receives the home as a joint owner, then he will receive both the home *and* his percentage interest as set forth in the will. Mary may believe John will share the property with his siblings after Mary dies, but John has no legal obligation to do so. If John does choose to share, then he will be making a gift and will be subject to filing a gift tax return. As illustrated with just this one piece of property, Mary has complicated her estate plan and, in fact, may have left some of the planning decisions and consequences to John.

Mary may have other options that would satisfy her goals without complication. Harry should have discussed Mary's assets and how they were titled and then shared the other solutions available so Mary could still avoid probate, eliminate tax problems, and leave her property to all of her children as she originally intended.

Mary also added John's name to her money market account. She reasoned it was for convenience in the event he needed to pay bills on her behalf. However, some of the same problems exist for the money market account as exist for the home. Again, the account is subject to John's creditors, and John will be the sole owner of the account when Mary dies – an outcome not consistent with the percentage distribution Mary made to her other children in her will. In fact, every time you put another person on one of your accounts or add a beneficiary to an account or life insurance, you are potentially creating a conflict with the estate plan you have in place. With proper advice, Mary could have enjoyed the same convenience without thwarting her own estate plan. Mary's better choice would have been to name John as one of her agents in her financial power of attorney.

As we mentioned in Chapter Three, Mary should have not just a will but a health care power of attorney, a HIPAA medical records authorization, a living will and a financial power of attorney. This ensures Mary will have assistance both with her legal and financial decisions as well as with her health care decisions in the event of her mental disability. A last will provides no lifetime benefits to Mary should she become mentally disabled.

A review of Mary's life insurance reveals that John and Susan are the named beneficiaries. Mary was a school teacher and purchased this life insurance policy many, many years ago, after Susan was born. When Robert was born, she never gave her life insurance beneficiary designation another thought. This is not unusual. Unfortunately, however, Robert may feel very left out when he realizes he was not named as a beneficiary of Mary's life insurance policy and has no legal right to any share.

Finally, all three children are named as equal beneficiaries on Mary's traditional IRA account. When Mary dies, each child will receive their one-third share, along with the taxes due on the distribution.

As a result of Mary's decisions regarding her home, her money market account, her life insurance and her IRA account, Mary's actual distribution to her children will be very different than what she intended through the terms of her last will. The chart below shows what Mary's children will actually receive versus the distribution Mary wanted.

Actual Distribution to Children		Distribution Mary Wanted
$545,000	John (35%)	$355,250
$260,000	Susan (35%)	$355,250
$210,000	Robert (30%)	$304,500

John will get the entire home, all of the funds in the money market account, half the life insurance death benefits, and one third of the IRA account. Susan will receive half the life insurance death benefits and one third of the IRA account. Robert will get just one third of the IRA account. Clearly this is not the result Mary wanted.

The fact is Mary's will doesn't work at all and is completely irrelevant, except for the fact it names her personal representative. All of Mary's assets will pass, not by the terms of her will, but as a result of joint ownership or beneficiary designations. The will Harry Hurry prepared wasn't worth the $250.00 Mary paid. His failure to discover the nature and ownership of her assets resulted in significant exposure to John's creditors, unexpected capital gains taxes, potential gift tax consequences or penalties, and a complete failure to benefit her children in the manner Mary intended. Although $250 appeared to be a good deal, it was actually a waste of money.

When you are ready to create your estate plan, find an experienced attorney who will educate and counsel you so your plan works the way you want. Don't attempt to use an online will creation service, a form from an office supply store or the least expensive attorney you can find.

If you believe your children or your heirs will all get along and work everything out as you desire, take it from us – it doesn't always happen that way. Once, Debbie received a call from Barbara, a woman in another state whose father, Steve, had recently died while living in Florida. Steve was 83 years old, loved both his son Bob, and his daughter Barbara and wanted his children to share equally in his estate when he died. Unfortunately, like many people, he did not understand how to make sure his wishes would be followed.

When Steve lived in Massachusetts, he prepared a will that left all his assets equally to Barbara and Bob. He later moved to Florida to live in the same town as Bob. Eventually, Steve sold his house in Massachusetts so he could build a house in his new hometown in Florida. In 2006, Steve built his house on a lot owned by Bob's girlfriend. He spent more than $100,000 improving a lot owned by someone else. Later Bob purchased the lot from his girlfriend and as a result, Bob now owns Steve's house.

After Steve built his house, Bob moved in. Steve put Bob's name on two of his accounts, and because of their cohabitation, Bob now has full access to all of Steve's papers. What Bob will share with his sister now that their father has died is debatable. Barbara suspects he will be unwilling to share any information. Bob is driving Steve's car and claims to be selling Steve's personal property – without Barbara's permission. Barbara has no choice but to retain an attorney to determine what her rights are with respect to her father's property. Unfortunately, Steve was either misinformed when he created his estate plan and believed it would work or he trusted Bob to share with his sister. In either event, it is not looking like Steve's plan will work the way he intended.

You have the power to create the plan you want, for yourself and your loved ones. If you fail to plan, your state Legislature has a plan for you. If you own your assets inconsistent with your plan, it is doomed to fail. Remember, if you fail to plan, you have planned to fail.

CHAPTER FIVE
CAN YOU TRUST YOUR FAMILY?

Love all, trust a few.
~ Shakespeare

A living trust is an estate planning directive that allows you to control your assets while you are alive and well, plan for yourself and your loved ones in the event of your mental disability and then give what you have, to whom you want, when you want, the way you want.

Trusts are essentially three-party contracts where you get to be all three parties while you are alive and well. You are the trustmaker (grantor/settler/trustor), the trustee (the person responsible for the daily investment, administration and distribution of trust assets) and the beneficiary during your lifetime. At the end of your lifetime, your trust assets will avoid probate, can save estate taxes and can continue to benefit your family for generations to come.

The benefits of having a fully funded trust and leaving your inheritance in trust for your spouse, children or other heirs are numerous. With a trust, you can:

- Provide continuity in the handling of your affairs by more efficiently transferring your property to your loved ones.

- Provide comfort to your loved ones during their period of grief and spare them unnecessary emotional or financial hardship should you become incapacitated and at the time of your death.

- Allow your family to avoid probate on your death, and avoid court guardianship proceedings on your disability, for all assets owned or controlled by your trust.

- Provide prenuptial protection for your spouse and children should your surviving spouse choose to remarry after your death – it can help assure your estate passes to your children and not to the new spouse.

- Ensure your trust easily moves with you from state to state.

- Create trusts for minor children and children who are disabled that are free from the supervision of the probate court. A special needs trust will also ensure no loss of government benefits.

- Retain control over your minor child's inheritance, rather than allowing the inheritance to get into the hands of your ex-spouse or the guardianship court. In a guardianship, the court is required to distribute all funds directly to the child at age 18, a result you may not want.

- Create trusts for adult children for the purpose of providing them with divorce protection, creditor protection and if necessary, protection from themselves if they have a drug, alcohol, chemical dependency disorder, a gambling addiction or they are incarcerated. Trusts can also protect adult children from carelessly spending their inheritance – an ailment commonly known as "affluenza."

- Protect an unmarried partner at the time of your death to ensure assets are protected for their benefit while allowing you to direct the distribution of remaining trust assets at the death of your partner.

- Guarantee the "stretch out" of your IRA benefits and the maximization of benefits to the family while minimizing income tax consequences.

- Help assure your family's privacy following your disability and death.

- Protect your children's inheritance from a step-parent if you should you die before your spouse.

- Achieve your death tax objectives by reducing or avoiding estate tax.

- Reduce after-death administrative expenses.

- Assure your trust assets will pass to the individuals you choose.

- Pass assets more quickly to your loved ones upon your death, avoiding some of the delays, hassles, and paperwork involved in the probate process.

- Provide peace of mind for yourself now and for your family later.

As you can see, a living trust based plan has many benefits. Trusts are often misunderstood and some people believe too complex. Our experience has been just the opposite – a well drafted trust, fully funded with the trustmaker's assets or named as beneficiary, can provide significant opportunities and avoid future problems.

Trusts come in many varieties – revocable living trusts, irrevocable trusts, charitable trusts, trust for business purposes, trusts for gift or estate tax purposes, trusts for long term care asset protection planning purposes – it can all become overwhelming. Most advanced planning techniques are beyond the scope of this book. Be sure to consult with your estate planning professional for guidance on advanced planning trust techniques and get all the education and information you need before making a decision.

CHAPTER SIX
SPECIAL PLANNING

Unmarried Partners and Same Sex Couples

Unmarried partners, either same sex or opposite sex provide interesting planning opportunities, along with some challenges. You can't just plug in what you know about planning for married couples or planning for single individuals. The rules are definitely different for couples who are in a committed but unmarried relationship.

Unmarried couples have a lot of the same concerns as married couples but very few of the protections afforded married couples under the law. In fact, there are more than 1,500 rights a person gains when they get married that are not available to singles. Peggy was in a long term unmarried relationship with her now husband, Joe. Without proper planning, Joe would not have the ability to make legal, financial or health care decisions on her behalf. It was essential for Peggy and Joe to prepare the appropriate legal directives – financial durable powers of attorney, health care powers of attorney and living wills. In addition, a trust plan was appropriate so they could protect each other (and their pets) in the event of a mental disability and at death.

Unmarried couples can't take advantage of unlimited lifetime and death gifting opportunities. As a result, unmarried partners must carefully monitor gifting between themselves to avoid gift tax reporting consequences and unintentionally using their lifetime gift exclusion. Simply owning an asset jointly can create an unexpected or unintended gift.

State laws favor the married status of couples. Unmarried couples have no rights under family law statutes and are rarely a preference under probate or health care statutes. Estate and gift tax laws are also unfavorable for unmarried partners. In a few instances, there may be tax advantages for the succession of business interests but those opportunities are limited.

An unmarried partner has no rights in the property of a deceased partner unless created by will or trust or in the form of ownership such as joint tenants with rights of survivorship. Retirement plan laws don't protect unmarried couples. The Social Security system and its laws provide no protection for the surviving partner in the event of death. If one partner gives up their career and no longer pays into Social Security, they may also be giving up rights related to disability and retirement.

Planning for unmarried couples and same sex partners requires attention to many different areas of the law. Be sure to consult with a qualified professional before undertaking planning on your own. For more information, pick up a copy of Peggy's book, *Loving Without a License – An Estate Planning Survival Guide for Unmarried Couples and Same Sex Partners,* available at LovingWithoutALicense.com or on Amazon.com.

Special Family Members

Many families who have loved ones with special needs rely on SSI, Medicaid or other needs-based government benefits to provide food, clothing, shelter and basic medical care. The assistance available could be dependent upon the state where you live. If you are a family with a special person, you undoubtedly know that while these State and Federal public benefits are very valuable, more is needed for your special person to fully enjoy life.

Ensuring your special person is well provided for without jeopardizing benefits can seem impossible. Unfortunately, most "plans" fail either because families try to cut corners and do it themselves or they don't work with someone who has expertise in this area of the law.

Some families are advised to disinherit their special family member — the very person who needs their help the most! This "solution" simply does not allow you to help your special person if you become incapacitated and when you die. Some families procrastinate, believing that today or even tomorrow is not the day they will become incapacitated or die – the "not me, not now" syndrome. The rule we prefer is, "It's never too early to plan, and you never know when it's going to be too late."

Some families believe they can rely on the kindness of other family members to provide financially for a disabled special person. We often see beneficiary designations on retirement plans and insurance policies that name another family member with the idea that the other family member will always provide for the special person. The reality is, you can't control what other family members will do with the money, and they will have no legal obligation to provide for the special person. In addition, unexpected occurrences for that other family member, such as divorce, creditor issues, incapacity, and death can completely change the outcome you've intended. Rather than rely on others to provide and plan for your special person after you're gone, get your own good advice, do your own planning, and consider your best possible solution – a properly drafted Special Needs Trust.

The primary purpose of a Special Needs Trust is to maintain your special person's eligibility for needs-based state and federal benefits while preserving adequate funds for additional needs not provided by government programs. Funds held by a Special Needs Trust do not count toward resource eligibility requirements, so the Special Needs Trust can pay for items not provided by public benefits without jeopardizing your special person's eligibility for those benefits. That is, the Special Needs Trust can provide funds to enhance your special person's life. Items the Special Needs Trust can provide include medications, medical equipment and therapies not covered by Medicare or Medicaid; educational and vocational programs; transportation; hobbies, sports, recreation and entertainment; travel for medical or recreational purposes; and possibly a personal assistant or care manager; to name a few.

A Special Needs Trust provides a benefit for other family members as well. Without a Special Needs Trust, your special person may receive a gift or an inheritance outright from someone who does not understand that the gift or inheritance could jeopardize continued eligibility for the benefits. With a Special Needs Trust, family members and friends can make lifetime or testamentary gifts directly to the Trust without causing a loss of benefits.

With a Special Needs Trust, you preserve government benefits, you can still call upon your family members to assist in ways they are most helpful, you protect the funds from creditors and divorce, you choose who will serve as trustee and as advisors, and you provide clear instructions with a helpful structure. By doing so, you lessen the burden on all family members and yet promote a loving, involved and supportive relationship among them. A Special Needs Trust is one of the most valuable gifts you can give your special needs person. For more information, read Peggy's book, *Special People, Special Planning –*

Creating a Safe Legal Haven for Families with Special Needs, available at SpecialPeopleSpecialPlanning.com or at Amazon.com.

Pets are Family, Too!

We are passionate about pets and believe pets are family, too! Peggy has no two-legged children, just the kind with four legs and fur coats - currently three horses, six dogs and four cats! Including your pets as part of your estate plan should be as natural as planning for your two-legged children. Pets can't take care of themselves so we have to give special consideration to their needs in the event of our disability and at our death.

Annabelle's Story

My name is Annabelle, and I'm lonely and scared. Yesterday morning, my friend and I went for our usual run. Then she fed me, filled my water bowl, and brushed me before going off to work. Now it's dark again . . . for the second time.

My friend is usually home before dark, and I'm always so glad to see her. She hugs me and takes good care of me. She feeds me again and we play in the backyard or walk to her boyfriend's house before going to bed.

I'm so hungry, and all my water is gone. Why isn't my friend home?! Does anyone know I'm here . . . alone? I've been barking but nobody has come, and now I'm just too tired to bark anymore. I'm scared. What's going to happen to me?

Wait, I hear someone at the door, yippee . . . but it's not my friend—I don't know who these people are. They're carrying a cage and coming towards me. Where are they taking me? Oh why did my friend leave me?!

We don't know what happened to Annabelle's friend, but the possibilities are limited only by our imagination. She may have been seriously injured in an auto accident or, worse yet, she may have died. She may have been the victim of a violent crime or stricken with a sudden, serious illness. We don't like to think that any of these things will happen to us, but the truth is, today could be our turn to be that "someone else" these things usually happen to.

Despite their short life expectancy, your pet may very well outlive you, or you may become disabled. If you don't come home today, would someone you trust

- Remember your pet and know how to gain access to your home?

- Know your pet's feeding schedule and other routines?

- Know how to find and administer your pet's medication?

- Be willing to take your pet home or find a new permanent loving home?

- Have the time and financial resources to care for your pet?

Planning for the care of your pet will give you peace of mind, knowing your pet will receive love and proper care in the event of your disability and at your death. Without planning, your pet may be left to the mercy of those who have little or no affection for your pet. Peggy had one client whose children simply opened the door and released her three dogs to the world, expecting them to fend for themselves or find a new home. Undoubtedly their lives came to an unexpected cross road, and we have no way of knowing how their story ended.

If you do nothing else, talk to the person or persons you believe will care for your pets should something happen to you, and make sure they are willing and have the financial resources to care for your pet. Make sure they know how to get into your home and how to access information about the care of your pets.

If you wish to do more, a Pet Trust is your best planning solution. It will ensure the right person will care for your pet, provide sufficient funds for lifetime care and appoint a trustee to make sure your instructions are carried out.

With a Pet Trust, you:

- Choose your pet's future caregiver;

- Provide financially for the care of your pet;

- Provide information about your pet that only you may know;

- Provide directions for such things as health care, exercise and recreation, diet and nutrition, and end-of-life decisions; and

- Ensure remaining funds to go to a charity, friend or family member.

Keep in mind that unwritten agreements with family or friends often go awry, because

- Emotions, personal circumstances and who we trust can change.

- Money left outright may go not for the care of your pet, but to possible creditors, a former spouse or any other unforeseen situation.

Finally, consider developing a relationship with a reliable pet sitter. Make your choice before an emergency occurs. Even if you have family nearby, they will appreciate having assistance with your pet while they are caring or grieving for you. Having someone who knows your pet and your routine will help greatly when making the transition to your substitute pet caregiver.

Animal Care Trust can provide trustee services for you and your pet. It's the only trustee program solely dedicated to the needs of pet owners and their pets. We've created Animal Care Trust to provide the investment and administrative oversight necessary to ensure your pets are taken care of for the rest of their lives. For more information, visit AnimalCareTrust.com.

For more information about planning for your pet, read *All My Children Wear Fur Coats – How to Leave a Legacy for Your Pet*, available at LegacyForYourPet.com or at Amazon.com.

CHAPTER SEVEN
HERE COMES THE TAX MAN –
BUT ESTATE PLANNING IS NOT JUST ABOUT TAXES

"I'm proud to be paying taxes in the United States.
The only thing is — I could be just as proud for half the money."
~ Arthur Godfrey

There are three main categories of taxes that may be triggered when dealing with wills, trusts and assets transferred during lifetime or at death. The categories are:

• Income taxes, which includes taxes on earned income, investment income and capital gains (or losses)

• Gift taxes

• Estate taxes, called inheritance taxes or estate transfer taxes in some states, and which can include generation-skipping taxes

Whether you or your estate are subject to one or all areas of these taxes depends on many factors such as your income tax bracket, whether you are married or single (including unmarried couples), whether you live in a community or separate property state, your net worth at your death, whether your state taxes transfers of assets at death in addition to the federal estate taxes that might be due, and other considerations such as how trust provisions are drafted, how assets are titled and ultimately, how your estate will be administered.

Tax planning can be complex and challenging. The rules change frequently and courts give conflicting interpretations of the rules. Some advisors focus their practice on tax planning and, indeed, some advisors and their clients can let the tax tail wag the estate planning dog. Essentially what that means is your estate plan shouldn't bc all about taxes – they are but one consideration in creating your overall plan.

If you have a general understanding of the three main categories of taxes, you will be in a better position to understand the recommendations your advisors might offer and then make good decisions about how you want to structure your estate plan. Failure to consider the tax consequences of gifts you make during your lifetime and at death, acquisitions or disposal of assets and other factors can cause you or your survivors to pay more taxes than necessary. Smart planning within the rules will allow you to utilize more assets during your lifetime and increase the value of assets for your loved ones at your death.

As mentioned, tax rules change regularly and the interpretations of these rules are dynamic. So it's important to regularly update your plan to make sure it stays current with your goals, circumstances, tax laws and your net worth. Only a plan kept current will allow you to take advantage of planning opportunities and avoid dangers for yourself and your loved ones.

Income Taxes

Assets held for investment can be invested for growth and/or income. Assets sold at a gain or loss will be subject to income tax rules regarding the gain or loss. If a trust is involved, the income tax might be attributable to the trustmaker or to the trust itself, depending on the terms of the trust. The general rule is that "grantor trusts," where the trustmaker is the trustee, are taxed to the trustmaker at his or her individual tax rates.

If the trustmaker has given up sufficient control over the trust, as in the case of an irrevocable trust, the income is generally taxed to the trust as a separate entity. Income taxed at trust tax rates often results in higher taxes than if taxed at individual tax rates. However, there may be compelling reasons why a person might opt to assume higher tax rates under a trust rather than the lower individual rates. These reasons generally relate to increased protections from other categories of taxes, increased creditor protections or other desired planning goals.

An often overlooked area of taxes is the capital gains tax. There are two considerations – one has to do with lifetime gifts and the other with gifts made at the time of death. A gift made during lifetime will transfer the donor's original basis (the price they paid for the gifted item). As a result, if you paid $1,000 for a painting and gifted it during your lifetime when it is worth $5,000, the individual receiving the gift has your original $1,000 basis and if they sell the painting for $5,000, they will have to pay capital gains tax on $4,000. If that same painting, however, were given at death, the recipient would receive what's called a "step up in basis." The receiver of the gift gets an increase in basis to the fair market value on the date of your death.

So the same painting received at death has a $5,000 basis and if sold for that same amount, the recipient will incur no capital gains tax at all. As you can see, the timing of gifts can be crucial to minimizing exposure to capital gains tax, especially on appreciated assets.

Gift Taxes

Under current gift tax rules, annual gifts of up to $13,000 (current figure) per person per year are excluded from your lifetime gift tax limit – currently $5,120,000. This means you may give as many gifts of $13,000 or less each year to as many individuals as you desire without incurring a gift tax obligation or an obligation to file a gift tax return. Married individuals can give unlimited gifts to each other and may join together and give up to $26,000 per year to others for the purposes of making annual exclusion gifts (this is called "gift splitting"). Certain other gifts may be made without using the $13,000 annual exclusion amount, but you should discuss those with your tax professional to make sure they are done correctly.

Annual gifts are one strategy to transfer assets from someone who has assets over the estate tax applicable exclusion amount (currently $5,120,000), or simply for the purpose of making lifetime gifts that can be enjoyed while the gift-giver is still alive and well. Consider that the estate tax applicable exclusion amount is generally subject to change every few years, so it is important to review your plan at least that often.

If you are concerned about gift taxes, it is important to coordinate your lifetime gifts with your probable distributions (gifts) at your death to avoid unnecessary taxes. If you anticipate having taxable gifts, you should work with your professional advisors to decide how to minimize your tax exposure.

Gifts made for the purpose of reducing a person's estate for Medicaid or VA planning purposes may be subject to reporting for IRS purposes. However, generally in the Medicaid and VA arena we aren't concerned about using a person's lifetime exemption. Be careful here – the rules related to Medicaid gifts are not the same as the rules for gifts for IRS purposes. A $13,000 gift from a Medicaid perspective may carry an eligibility penalty while the same gift from an IRS perspective is not taxable or reportable.

Estate Taxes

The obligation to pay estate taxes depends on the size of your estate. Currently, if an estate is less than $5,120,000 and death occurs in 2012, your estate will not have any liability for federal estate taxes. This can be a tricky area, however, for a number of reasons. First, people are not always clear about what is included in their taxable estate. Second, the estate tax exemption amount changes every few years.

Generally, we say everything you own, everything you control and everything with your name on it gets included for estate tax purposes. This means that all of your jointly held property gets included (at least a portion of it), everything you own individually, all your life insurance policies (not just the cash value but the death benefit value), your retirement plans including IRAs, 401ks, deferred compensation, and so forth are included.

The "estate tax applicable exclusion" amount, also known as the "estate tax exemption" amount, is the amount each person can leave free of estate taxes at death. As mentioned, it is currently $5,120,000 but that amount is scheduled to expire on December 31, 2012. As of this writing, that amount is slated to return to $1,000,000 as of January 1, 2013. Stay tuned, however, because this could change very quickly in our current political climate. Further, the estate tax exemption has changed frequently in recent years, making it absolutely essential to consult with a qualified tax planning professional.

Here's an example of what the estate tax exemption amount has been in recent years:

2005 - $1,500,000

2006 - $2,000,000

2007 - $2,000,000

2008 - $2,000,000

2009 - $3,500,000

2010 - $5,000,000 or $0

2011 - $5,000,000

2012 - $5,120,000

2013 - $1,000,000 (if nothing changes)

Estate taxes are essentially a voluntary tax in the sense that you can "volunteer" to pay them by failing to plan adequately. With proper planning, the estate taxes due on your death can be minimized or avoided. However, avoiding payment of unnecessary taxes requires education and planning. Seek out the advice of a qualified tax or legal professional to assist you in structuring your estate in a way that will minimize the estate tax effects on your estate and provide the maximum inheritance to your loved ones.

Generation skipping taxes are another level of tax that may be incurred when the trustmaker elects to "skip" a generation with regard to gifting. To skip a generation doesn't mean your children won't benefit from your assets, only that they won't be responsible for the payment of any associated estate tax. These estate taxes are deferred to future generations and must be paid upon distribution to the subsequent generations. Currently the generation skipping tax is unified with the estate tax and is currently at $5,120,000. Again, that number changes regularly.

Planning for generation skipping taxes is a complex area of the law, and consultation with your legal and tax professionals is highly recommended.

Tax law changes are an example of why estate plans must be updated. Although legal and financial advisors can create directives and build plans to withstand many of the anticipated changes in the law, your best interests are served if your estate plan is subjected to professional scrutiny from time to time.

It's Not Just About Taxes

Minimizing income, gift and estate taxes is an admirable goal, but it shouldn't be the only reason you do planning. Estate planning can accomplish many goals including the protection of yourself and your loved ones. Sometimes tax strategies create more complexity than families are prepared to deal with. Work with a professional who can listen to all of your goals and help you design a plan that best meets the needs of you and your family.

CHAPTER EIGHT
PROTECT YOUR ASS . . . ETS

"Leave your kids enough money so they would feel
they can do anything but not so much that they could do nothing."
~ *Warren Buffett*

Inheritance Protection for Your Loved Ones

Remember Mary . . . we introduced her and her three children to you in Chapter Four. When we left Mary, we saw how her assets will be distributed despite the instructions in her will. Fortunately, Mary is still healthy, so she can review her assets to make sure the ownership and beneficiary designations align with the wishes expressed in her will. However, that's not the end of her story.

It's important to talk with your estate planning attorney about your assets and how they are titled and who the beneficiaries are. It's equally important to talk with your attorney about your family – the good, the bad, and the ugly. Here's what we learn when we ask Mary a few more questions.

Mary's son, John has been a real estate investor for a number of years. Mary is not privy to all his holdings, but given the state of the economy since 2008, it is probable John will be facing a foreclosure or a short sale on one or more of his properties. While the residential rental market is beginning to thrive, there was a period when properties were difficult to rent and the rent didn't always cover the amount of the mortgage. The commercial real estate market continues to suffer. Since John may be facing current or impending creditors, if he receives an inheritance from Mary, that inheritance may go to pay John's creditors. What are Mary's options?

Mary's daughter, Susan has been in a difficult marriage for a long time. Susan is easily influenced by her husband but recently has been thinking about filing for divorce. If Susan receives an inheritance from Mary and co-mingles it with her marital assets by putting it in a joint account, it is likely Susan's husband will claim an ownership interest in at least half of the inheritance Susan receives from Mary. What are Mary's options?

Mary's son, Robert is a spendthrift. Robert likes to spend money, on everything – new cars, trips, clothes, electronics, good times on Saturday nights, and on his friends. More than a few times, Mary has helped him financially when his credit card balances were so high he couldn't make the payments or when he was in default on a car payment. If Robert receives an outright inheritance from Mary, it is likely the money won't be around for long. What are Mary's options?

Mary's children are an example of the difficulties any of our children might be facing today; and even if they don't currently have one of these problems, you never know when things are going to change. The financial crisis we are currently experiencing shows us that bad things can happen to good people. Some marriages don't last forever, and many view the receipt of an inheritance as "found money." Insurance companies tell us it doesn't matter how much someone receives or how old they are when they receive their inheritance, it's generally gone in nine to 18 months.

Worse, what if you have a child who has an addiction to drugs, alcohol or gambling? With proper planning, you have the tools to protect your child from himself or herself. Assets held in a continuing trust after death can provide lifetime protection to children and grandchildren. We call them lifetime protective trusts. Properly drafted, a lifetime protective trust can provide protection from creditors (John's potential problem), predators and "outlaws" (Susan's potential problem) and themselves (Robert's potential problem), while still providing access for everything necessary for a happy, healthy life – for health, education and maintenance.

For many of the advantages or trusts, please refer to Chapter Five. We like to say, "If you love me, leave it in trust." You'll be glad you did, and so will your kids.

Asset Protection for Yourself

In a world of creditors and predators and where we already know that bad things happen to good people, taking a look at your assets from an asset protection perspective is a good idea. Some assets have built-in asset protection under state laws. Others can have asset protection because of the nature of the asset or the way it is owned.

We've already learned from Mary's story that ownership as joint tenants with rights of survivorship doesn't provide any asset protection because it exposes the asset to the creditors of both owners. In some states, however, a husband and wife have a form of ownership known as tenants by the entireties. Property held as tenants by the entireties is protected from the claims of the creditors of one of the owners. So if one person causes an accident and was sued, any property owned as tenants by the entireties is protected. The creditor would have to have a claim against both owners to be successful. This works well while both owners are living but disappears in the event one of the owners should die.

Retirement plans like an Individual Retirement Account (IRA) or a 401k, annuities and the cash value of life insurance often have both built-in and state law protection from the claims of creditors. Homestead property may also have protection from creditors. In Florida, your home is your castle and is protected from your general creditors – but not your mortgage company, your homeowner's association or mechanic's liens. It's important to check the laws in your own state with respect to these assets because not all states protect all assets equally.

Limited liability companies and family limited partnerships may also provide protection from creditors. These entities will have specific operating requirements and the level of protection may vary from state to state. Generally, a creditor of one of the owners of a limited liability company or a limited partnership will only have the right to a charging order as his remedy against the debtor. This means the creditor would be entitled to distributions, if any were made, but would not have the right to foreclose their interest or make any decisions related to the operation of the entity.

Domestic asset protection trusts and off-shore trusts are other planning techniques used by individuals concerned about creditor protection. These trusts may have significant protections but must be carefully drafted pursuant to the applicable state law or the laws of the foreign jurisdiction. Generally they require a resident trustee and as a result may have significant ongoing operating costs. Most jurisdictions also require that you be creditor free at the time of creation and funding to avoid a claim of fraudulent conveyance by the creditor.

Another way of adding a layer of protection is with the use of sufficient liability insurance. Talk to your insurance professional about your net worth to make sure you have enough coverage. Many people believe a revocable living trust provides asset protection, but it doesn't – anything you can easily access is also accessible by your creditors. Overall, asset protection requires significant expertise and knowledge of many types of laws. You should never undertake asset protection planning without the guidance of an experienced practitioner.

Long Term Care Asset Protection Planning

Long term care asset protection planning is sometimes referred to as Medicaid planning. Most people believe they will never want or need Medicaid and we hope that's true. However, Medicaid is the only public payer for nursing home care in this country. As our country ages and the cost of nursing home care rises, it is likely someone you know or love will need the benefits of Medicaid.

Again, many people believe a revocable living trust provides the long term planning they need, but it doesn't. Your best defense against the rising cost of nursing home care is long term care insurance. It has been our experience, however, that many people wait too long and then can't qualify because of health issues or the cost has simply become too high. We encourage everyone to investigate long term care insurance early and then make an informed decision. Peggy obtained her long term care insurance while in her 40's – she was young, healthy and it was very affordable. Peggy's parents also have long term care insurance and it paid for her dad to be in a nursing home for almost two years before his death. As a result, Peggy's mom didn't have to worry about using family assets to provide for expensive care. Nursing homes cost approximately $6,500-$8,500 per month. An assisted living facility costs approximately $4,500-$6,500 per month. In home, 24-hour care for seven days a week can be as much as $12,000 per month. How long could you or your family write those checks before you ran out of money?

When a family doesn't have long term care insurance, Medicaid or the VA may be their only option for assistance. If you do your own investigation, you will find a lot of conflicting information, so we recommend you thoroughly educate yourself and seek out the services of a qualified elder law attorney before engaging in any long term care asset protection planning for yourself or a loved one. One of the biggest mistakes we see are well-meaning friends, family and other professionals providing guidance or advice that is inappropriate and illegal. In addition, the laws vary from state to state, so the advice you get from a syndicated newspaper column or person from another state is often wrong for your situation. There are also lots of myths surrounding planning techniques and what you have to do in order to qualify for benefits.

One commonly promoted myth is you have to spend all your assets before you can qualify for benefits. This is simply not true. Medicaid and VA do have income and asset limitations but there are many ways to accomplish your planning goals. It is the rare case where a family would be required to spend all their assets before qualifying for benefits. Gifting may be appropriate but can be especially problematic if Medicaid eligibility is your goal. Medicaid imposes a period of ineligibility for gifts made in the five years prior to application. However, with proper planning, this time period can be reduced or eliminated.

In some states your home and your vehicle are exempt assets. This means they don't count for eligibility purposes. However, many people believe that "Medicaid will take your home," and in most cases this is completely untrue. To avoid this potential result, many believe they need to sell their home. This can often create additional, unexpected problems because once the house is sold, the net cash proceeds are generally a countable resource. Transferring your home to your children doesn't fix the problem either, as the transfer is viewed as a gift.

Irrevocable burial contracts are often a good planning tool. It allows the family to take care of very important business in advance of need without any negative benefits consequences. Caregiver contracts, income producing real property, pooled trusts and other planning techniques may also be options, depending on your state and its rules.

Long term care protection planning should be carefully integrated with your estate plan. One cannot be accomplished without the other. State laws can impose unexpected consequences without proper planning. One example would be transferring all assets to one spouse (the well spouse) for the purpose of allowing the other spouse (the ill spouse) to qualify for Medicaid benefits. If the well spouse unexpectedly died first, without proper planning, all the assets may be transferred back to the ill spouse. This could result in a loss of benefits by the ill spouse. Trying to disinherit the ill spouse can also have unexpected results –

many states have elective share statutes that could require a surviving spouse on Medicaid to make a claim against the deceased spouse's estate. Your legal professional can tell you the options you have to protect the ill spouse from loss of benefits and still allow for a good quality of life.

If long term care asset protection planning sounds like Greek to you, you aren't alone. There are a lot of moving parts, all of which need to be orchestrated to achieve the best possible results – benefits for an individual who requires long term care while preserving assets for the benefit of a well spouse and possibly other family members.

CHAPTER NINE
ONE MORE CONVERSATION

"Children will not remember you for the material things you provided
but for the feeling that you cherished them."
~ Richard L. Evans

Imagine you are sitting comfortably in your favorite chair at home. You are thinking of a loved one who has died and remembering good times you had with him or her. *Really imagine it.* In one of your hands is your loved one's last will and testament. In your other hand is a letter your loved one wrote you before death, but was not delivered to you until after death. Which do you read first?

Have you ever wished for just "one more conversation" with a loved one who is gone? Most people do. The death of a loved one can come suddenly from a car accident, a stroke or heart attack, or it can come after a long illness such as cancer, but it is never something we are completely prepared for. Debbie's father died in 1998 after a stroke. She often recalls good times with her dad – time they spent sitting and talking, and it makes her sad to know she can never talk with him again. Photographs help us relive moments, but could there be something more?

What if you could have one last conversation with your loved one, over and over? Debbie was asked to review a strongbox that contained a friend's mother's estate papers. Debbie's friend had just learned her mother was very ill and was not expected to live much longer. Debbie reviewed the documents to determine if anything needed to be updated. The last paper she found, on the bottom of the strongbox, was a note from her friend's mother to her two children, telling them how much she loved them and how happy her life had been because of them. We believe that's the greatest legacy of all!

Nothing can take the place of a loved one, but when we leave a letter, a note or a story, we give those we leave behind the opportunity to have one more conversation with us, over and over again. When we leave a written remembrance, we leave a smile – a reason to cry happy tears. We can share the memory of a special time, moments or personal characteristics that we treasure, the depth of our love and our hopes and dreams for the future. So much can be accomplished with a simple note left for those we leave behind.

Peggy's dad always said he was going to write a book called, "Letters to My Children." Peggy was anxious for him to write this book because she is the oldest of four children and believed there would be many important messages for her. Her dad never wrote that book, but rather than lose the opportunity to have such a valuable communication, Peggy encouraged her dad to share poems, letters, speeches and sermons he had written during his lifetime. Peggy and her sister, Julie compiled these writings in a book entitled, *I Live but Once,* the same name as one of his poems. Her dad then wrote a personal note to each of his children on their own personal copy. In addition, the book served as a centerpiece for readings at her father's funeral a fter his death. This is just one example of other ways you can capture and preserve precious memories.

If you've experienced the need for one more conversation with a loved one you have lost, consider, too, that those who love you would enjoy such a gift from you. Your true legacy is, after all, who you are, not what you have. You have the opportunity to transfer your inner riches with purposeful intention. Your legal last will answers "What do I want my loved ones to have," while your last conversation answers "What do I want my loved ones to know?"

A life worth living is full of surprises, twists and turns. Your experiences can provide valuable lessons to those who come after you. Your experiences can help them understand who you are and help them avoid your mistakes and build on your successes. By sharing your experiences and perspective, a lifetime of wisdom can be passed along to future generations.

Words are powerful instruments, so be cautious. Your message will be carried by your loved ones for the rest of their lives. If it is a negative message, they may have difficulty adjusting to your death and to the rest of their life. At every word, recall the love you feel and try to turn any negative thoughts into a positive statement. For example, if you are disappointed your child never went to college, rather than say "I'm disappointed you never went to college," you might say "You have proven yourself to be responsible and with a strong work ethic. You have a beautiful family, and I am confident you will continue to grow as a person I would always be proud of." When we see positives in others, we help them see their own positives and grow.

When we speak a positive message, we believe those we leave behind will want to live up to those expectations. If we speak of love and pride, they will be left with love and pride in themselves, leading them to a path of prosperity and success. If the message is negative, they may well be left with a sadness that will follow them all the days of their life.

Here are some topics that may help you get started with your conversation:

- ♥ Never give up
- ♥ Look every day for something to be grateful for
- ♥ Faith in God is important
- ♥ Set aside time for play
- ♥ Learn to be honest and humble
- ♥ Be generous with love
- ♥ My hope for you is . . .
- ♥ I respect and admire you because . . .
- ♥ The best decision I ever made was . . .
- ♥ The worst decision I ever made was . . .
- ♥ The greatest influence on my life was . . .
- ♥ To me, success means . . .
- ♥ Mistakes I've learned from
- ♥ The hardest thing I ever had to do (and the way I dealt with it) was . . .
- ♥ At times of stress in my life, the thing that got me through it was . . .
- ♥ I was most proud of you when . . .
- ♥ My thoughts on
  - Education/Learning/Reading
  - Giving/Receiving
  - Respect
  - Gratitude

- Positive thinking
- Self-improvement
- Wealth and saving for the future
- Making mistakes
- Hope for the future

Here are some of the ways you might get started:

♥ I fully expect I will share many more years with you, but if for some reason that is not to be, there are some things I would like to make sure you always remember...

♥ Eventually, you're going to receive some of my property, but I like to think I am more than my money or property. I thought writing this would be a great way to reflect upon my intangible property and what makes me feel truly wealthy...

♥ My legal documents imply the love I hold for you, but they are not the last words I want you to have from me...

♥ I have a letter my mother wrote to me, and I treasure it to this day. This I write for you, so you may have your own treasure...

♥ I have made some decisions in my estate plan, and I don't want my decisions to be misinterpreted...

♥ By the time you are old enough to receive the assets in this trust, I will no longer be here to tell the story behind what you are inheriting...

♥ I once met a man who inspired me to always do my best, own up to my mistakes and make every moment in life count. I want to share what he taught me...

♥ The most important thing I can give you, I hope I already have – my love and belief in you as a person of great inner beauty and worth...

♥ Your ties to each other will be the longest you have. Support each other in good times and in bad...

♥ Be respectful of everyone you meet – most everyone can do something better than you…

♥ As I reflect on our life together, I feel nothing but gratitude for . . .

♥ My life wouldn't be the same without . . .

♥ The smell of my grandfather's garage . . .

♥ My mother introduced me to the joys of . . .

♥ When your father was a little boy, he . . .

♥ The reason these watches from my grandfather are so important to me is . . .

♥ It is my hope that the inheritance I am leaving will enable you to . . .

This is also a good time to make sure your loved ones know your true feelings, not only about them, but what you might need from them as well. Some of the things we may wish our family to know are:

♥ I would like to be forgiven for those times I hurt my family, friends and others.

♥ I would like to have my family, friends and others know I forgive them for when they may have hurt me.

♥ I would like my family and friends to know that I know I am loved.

♥ I would like my family and friends to know I do not fear death itself. I think it is not the end.

♥ I would like all of my family members to make peace with each other, if they can.

♥ I want my family, friends and caregivers to respect my wishes even if they don't agree with them.

♥ I want the memories of my life to give my friends and family joy and not sorrow.

We also believe gratitude is central to a life filled with joy. The simple act of saying "thank you" can have a dramatic effect not only on your recipient, but it can also change your life – *because what you send out always returns to you.* We believe you can attract joy and prosperity through acts of kindness and expressions of gratitude. If you would like to learn more about bringing gratitude into your life and how it can change your life and those you meet, please read our book, *Thank Everybody for Everything, Grow Your Life and Business with Gratitude,* found on Amazon.com.

We also created *Gratitude Expressions, a Five Year Journal* (also found at Amazon.com), for the purpose of memorializing on a daily basis what we are grateful for. It is a unique journal for recording, tracking and re-visiting your daily gratitude expressions over a five-year period. Using *Gratitude Expressions* on a daily basis can be a gift to your loved ones – a true legacy. We have both used and enjoyed our *Gratitude Expressions* journal for several years.

One of Debbie's friends is using the *Gratitude Expressions* journal to write something for her young daughter every day as she grows from childhood. She is committed to doing this every day for the entire five years. Do you think this will someday be a legacy her daughter will treasure? In fact, we believe it will become a special treasure shared by the two of them.

Let's go back to Mary's story for a moment. Remember Robert was going to receive less than his siblings? He was only going to receive 30% of Mary's estate, and his brother and sister were each to receive 35%. If Robert doesn't receive an explanation, what will he think? He will probably think his mother was disappointed in him or that she loved his brother and sister more, or that she just didn't love him at all. The truth is, Mary helped Robert financially over his lifetime due to his poor spending habits, and the distribution in her will is her way of trying to even things out for her other children.

We think it's important for Mary to share her intentions with Robert; and if she doesn't feel comfortable doing so before her death, we would suggest she write a letter for Robert to receive after her death. In her letter, we believe Mary should not only explain her intentions but share her love for Robert. Of course, if she is going to do that for Robert, it makes sense for her to also do it for John and Susan, so their feelings are not hurt as well.

We believe every time a person dies, it's like a library burning down – the history and special memories of that individual are lost forever. If you want more ideas on how to leave a legacy for your family, read *Like a Library Burning – Saving and Sharing Stories of a Lifetime* by Peggy and friend, Scott Farnsworth, available on Amazon.com.

Remember, after we die, we live on in the hearts and minds of others. Your legacy is your love – share it!

"Thousands of candles can be lighted from a single candle,
and the life of the candle will not be shortened.
Happiness never decreases by being shared."
~ Buddha

CHAPTER TEN
WHAT TO DO WHEN SOMEONE DIES

Never say you know a man
until you have divided an inheritance with him.
~ Johann Kasper Lavater

Prudent planning is all about making sure you have a plan that works the way you wish, so you may have peace of mind now, and your family may have peace of mind when you are gone. After all, once you're gone, there is no fixing a broken plan.

Whether you die with just a will or a will and a trust, there will be work to be done after your death. While most people are anxious to avoid probate and attempt to use trusts to avoid the probate process, we often see trusts that are unfunded, meaning there are few, if any, assets titled in the name of the trust. In that case, some form of probate is inevitable. Of course, we have met many people like Mary who do other things to avoid probate, often with disastrous results for the family.

A will becomes effective upon death and controls only property that is owned individually (i.e., property that is not owned jointly with another or property that has no beneficiary designation). In your will, you select a personal representative or executor to administer your probate estate after your death. The court then supervises the activity of the personal representative and the administration of your estate. It is probably this court oversight that causes people to say probate costs too much, takes too long, and is a too public a process. We believe probate can actually have some significant advantages – court oversight being one. A second advantage is the process for identifying and paying creditors – this time period may be considerably shorter than waiting for a state's creditor claim period to run. In Florida, without a probate administration, creditors have two years to file claims against an estate.

If you die with individually owned assets, whether you die with a will or without a will, your estate will be subject to probate. There are essentially three steps in the probate process: (1) gather and value the assets of the estate, (2) identify and pay the creditors of the estate (including attorney fees and personal representative fees), and (3) distribute the remaining assets to the beneficiaries (as set forth in your will or determined by your state's intestate succession rules). The probate court will oversee each of these steps to ensure they are done properly and timely.

If you own assets in more than one state, you may have more than one probate – one for each state where you own property. This may significantly increase the expense and time delays given the need to maneuver through each state's probate process and the hiring of legal counsel in each jurisdiction.

Trusts are effective when signed and control only the property owned by the trust or the property where the trust is named as beneficiary. With an unfunded trust, you may have both probate administration and trust administration, resulting in unmet expectations by the successor trustee or beneficiaries.

A trust names a successor trustee to take over the administration of the trust upon your death. You may also name a successor trustee to step in if you become mentally incompetent. The administration of your trust after death is private, but your trustee is still responsible for paying your debts, the expenses of trust administration (including attorney fees and trustee fees) and the gathering and distribution of assets according to your trust. This privacy factor can also result in unexpected consequences because untrained successor trustees may not be familiar with state trust laws and may, therefore, administer the estate improperly. Family members may be hesitant to pursue legal action either because they want to avoid family disharmony or they aren't aware there has been a breach of fiduciary responsibility.

When you consider the cost of administration after death, whether in a probate or trust administration, it is important to also consider the overall cost of estate planning. What you spend on estate planning can directly impact the cost of probate or trust administration. Of course, there's the initial cost of planning. Mary paid $250.00 for a will, yet Harry Hurry (her attorney) had no knowledge about her assets, her family or her true wishes – he gave her a plan that was destined to fail. The $250.00 Mary paid was wasted, because Mary didn't receive the plan she wanted. As a result, the cost to Mary's family, if she does not do proper planning now, will be significant.

Remember Steve and his two children, Barbara and Bob from Chapter Four? He did his planning in New Jersey and never thought about updating. Many people think estate planning is a "one and done." Nothing could be further from the truth. The average person updates his or her plan every 19.6 years. Has anything in your life changed in the last 20 years? It is likely in that time span, you may have moved, a loved one has died or become incapacitated, someone got married or a child was born. In addition, laws have changed and there's a good chance the expertise of your professional advisor has changed (hopefully improved) as well.

With so many possible changes, it only makes sense to keep your plan updated and relevant to your current situation. If Steve had met with a knowledgeable attorney every few years who reviewed his assets, including the title to his home, he would have learned the plan he created would not work.

Debbie was contacted by a woman who wanted her father's will reviewed to make sure it said what he wished. They both came in and the will, in fact, said exactly what the father wanted – to leave all his property to his two children equally. Then Debbie asked about assets. The father stated he had two accounts - on one both children were account owners with their father, but on the other, only the son was a joint account owner. There was $68,000 in the account with just the son's name. As a result, the daughter was not guaranteed to receive the $34,000 her father intended for her benefit. Upon learning this result, the father became upset and had to change the account ownership. He thought his will controlled everything, but it didn't.

The cost of estate planning is not just the cost after death – probate, trust administration, legal fees, personal representative or trustees fees, accounting fees, appraisal fees and taxes, to name a few. It's also the initial cost (what you paid the first time you did your planning) and ultimately, the cost of keeping your plan updated over time. In some instances, the failure to keep a plan updated can result in a total failure of the plan – thereby resulting in a loss of 100% of the estate assets. An even bigger cost can be the emotional cost of destroyed family relationships if the plan doesn't work as intended.

Other costs include final expenses related to the disposition of our body – burial or cremation and memorial services. In many states, your heirs have the right to decide whether you are buried or cremated, regardless of the instructions you leave in your will or otherwise.

You have the option, however, to preplan your burial or cremation and memorial services. While preplanning will not guarantee your heirs won't still go against your wishes, they may think long and hard about spending additional money and depleting their inheritance.

If you have lost a loved one, you should gather a team to advise you. This team might consist of an attorney, a certified public accountant, a financial advisor, trusted friends and perhaps a professional trustee. Generally, we recommend the following:

- Allow yourself the time and luxury to grieve.

- Complete funeral and memorial service arrangements.

- Contact immediate family and friends.

- Locate estate planning documents (these will become your Operating Manual).

- Locate asset and creditor information.

- Arrange for the care of surviving family and pets.

- Secure real and personal property.

- Read your Operating Manual.

- Gather your Professional Team

There are certain things you don't want to do, and your attorney will be able to properly advise you on those issues. Many of these relate to maximizing estate tax benefits. Your attorney will also be able to advise you on proper notifications to make to governmental agencies and organizations, and also help you with the inventory of assets, identification of creditors, priority of debt payments, and identification of, and distribution to beneficiaries.

As personal representative or trustee, you have a fiduciary responsibility to:

- Comply with the terms of the will or trust

- Comply with the laws relating to wills and trusts

- Be fair in dealings with creditors and beneficiaries

- Comply with tax requirements

- Segregate, preserve and invest estate or trust assets

- Keep and render a full and accurate record and accounting of estate and/or trust assets

Probate administration generally ends when the judge has concluded the personal representative has completed his or her responsibilities, including the distribution of assets. Trust administration concludes pursuant to the terms of the trust document – it may be upon outright distribution, or upon distribution when the beneficiaries reach certain ages, when administration is too expensive so as to become "burdensome," or not for many generations.

When considering your own plan, review asset ownership and beneficiary designations and how they integrate with your overall goal and plan. Make sure your plan nominates those individuals or organizations with the greatest opportunity to succeed as personal representative or successor trustee. Keep your plan current and relevant to your life's ever-changing situation. Tell your loved ones how much they mean to you by leaving a heart-felt letter that will allow them their last conversation with you – over and over again.

Co-create your plan with counseling-oriented planning partners. Commit yourself and your family to a formal lifetime maintenance and education program. Keep your documents and assets organized and tell your loved ones where they can locate important documents in the event of your incapacity and death. Lastly, secure appropriate assistance for you and your loved ones through the development of a strong relationship with a legal professional to assure your wisdom is transferred along with the rest of your wealth.

What we have done for ourselves alone dies with us;
what we have done for others and the world remains and is immortal.
~Albert Pike

Appendix A

GLOSSARY OF ESTATE PLANNING TERMS

Administrator: Person named in your will and appointed by the court to administer your probate estate. Also called an Executor or Personal Representative.

Agent: An individual named in a power of attorney with authority to act on the power giver's behalf. Has a fiduciary responsibility to the power giver. Sometimes called Attorney-in-Fact.

Ancillary Administration: An additional probate in another state. Typically required when you own assets or real estate in a state other than the state where you live that is not titled in the name of your trust or in the name of a joint owner with rights of survivorship.

Applicable Exclusion Amount: The amount of property owned by a decedent effectively exempt from the federal estate and gift tax ($5,120,000 in 2012).

Attorney-in-Fact: An individual named in a power of attorney with authority to act on the power giver's behalf. Has a fiduciary responsibility to the power giver. Sometimes called an Agent.

Basis: What you paid for an asset. Value used to determine gain or loss for capital gains and income tax purposes.

Beneficiary: The person named in a will or trust to receive or benefit from property owned by the maker of the Will or grantor of a Trust. During lifetime, a trust grantor may be a beneficiary.

Buy-Sell Agreement: A written agreement between co-owners of a business to determine the rights of the owners in the event of retirement, termination, bankruptcy, divorce, disability or death.

Capacity: The legal competence to effectively perform a given act (e.g., to write a Will or Trust or enter into a binding contract).

Co-Trustees: Two or more individuals who have been named to act together in managing a trust's assets. A Corporate Trustee can also be a Co-Trustee.

Corporate Trustee: An institution, such as a bank, trust company, or charitable organization that specializes in managing or administering trusts.

Decedent: A person who has died.

Disclaim: To refuse to accept a gift or inheritance so it may be transferred to the next recipient in line. Currently must be done within nine months of the date-of-death to be tax qualified. Sometimes referred to as a "legal no thank you."

Durable Power of Attorney for Financial Matters: A legal document that gives another person full or limited legal authority to make financial and property decisions on your behalf. May be effective immediately or be "springing" depending on your jurisdiction. Valid through mental incapacity or disability. Ends upon revocation, adjudication of incapacity, and death.

Durable Power of Attorney for Healthcare: A legal document that gives another person legal authority to make health care decisions for you if you are unable to make them for yourself. Also called Healthcare Proxy, Healthcare Surrogate or Medical Power of Attorney.

Estate Administration: The process of settling either a probate estate or trust estate. There are generally three steps that include identifying the assets, paying the debts of the estate and distributing the balance to the beneficiaries.

Executor/Executrix: The one nominated in a Will and thereafter appointed by the Probate Court to manage and distribute a decedent's estate in accordance with the terms of the Will. Also known as a Personal Representative.

Fiduciary: Person or entity having the legal duty to act for another person's benefit and occupying a position of trust and accountability. Requires great confidence, trust, and a high degree of good faith. Usually associated with a Trustee, Personal Representative, Executor, Guardian, Conservator).

Funding: The process of re-titling and transferring your assets to your Living Trust. Also includes the re-designation of beneficiaries to include your Living Trust as a beneficiary. Sometimes called asset integration.

Generation Skipping Transfer (GST) Tax: A federal tax imposed on certain transfers, either by gift during life or at death, between a donor/decedent and a person more than one generation removed (e.g., a grandchild).

Gift Tax: Federal tax on completed lifetime gifts made from one person to another. The current lifetime exclusion amount is $5,120,000 for 2012. The current annual exclusion amount is $13,000. May require tax reporting to the IRS on Form 709.

Grantor: The person who establishes a trust. Also referred to as the "Trustor," "Trustmaker" or "Settlor."

Gross Estate: The total value, for estate tax purposes, of everything in which one has an ownership interest at the time of death.

Guardian: an individual or professional appointed by the Guardianship Court to be responsible for the person or property of a Ward.

Guardianship: A court supervised proceeding whereby after evaluation and review a Guardian is appointed to act on behalf of a minor or incapacitated person (the Ward). A Guardian must be appointed if the incapacitated person did not designate an agent or surrogate in a Durable Power of Attorney (for financial and health care matters) while he or she was competent.

Heir: The person entitled to distribution of an asset or property interest under applicable state law in the absence of a Will. The terms "heir" and "beneficiary" are not synonymous.

Health Care Proxy: A legal document that gives another person legal authority to make health care decisions for you if you are unable to make them for yourself. Also called Durable Power of Attorney for Healthcare, Healthcare Surrogate or Medical Power of Attorney.

Inter vivos: Latin term that means "between the living." An *inter vivos* trust is created while you are living instead of after you die. A Revocable Living Trust is an *inter vivos* trust.

Intestate/Intestacy: When a person dies without a valid will, his or her estate is distributed pursuant to state intestacy laws.

Irrevocable Life Insurance Trust (ILIT): An irrevocable trust for the purpose of holding title to life insurance. Used as an advance planning technique to remove the death benefit proceeds of a life insurance policy from an insured's gross taxable estate. Can be used to take advantage of annual exclusion gifts.

Irrevocable Trust: A trust that cannot be changed, amended or canceled once it is created. Opposite of Revocable Living Trust. Can be created during lifetime or after death.

Intestate: Dying without a Will.

Joint Ownership: When two or more persons own the same asset, either as tenants in common or as joint tenants with right of survivorship.

Joint Tenants with Right of Survivorship: A form of joint ownership where the deceased owner's share automatically and immediately transfers to the surviving joint tenant(s) or owner(s).

Living Trust: A legal entity created during your life, to which you transfer ownership of your assets. Contains your instructions to control and manage your assets while you are alive and well, plan for you and your loved ones in the event of your mental disability and give what you have, to whom you want, when you want, the way you want at your death. Avoids guardianship of property and avoids probate only if fully funded at incapacity and/or death. Also called a Revocable Inter Vivos Trust.

Life Alliance Agreement: A written agreement between two life partners for the purpose of establishing ownership to property, rights and obligations with regard to property and disposition of property in the event of the termination of the relationship.

Life Alliance Partner: A life partner of the same or opposite-sex in a committed, but unmarried, relationship.

Limited Liability Company (LLC): A form of legal entity that can provide limited liability from the claims of creditors. Can be taxed as a sole proprietorship, partnership, s-corporation or c-corporation.

Living Will: A legal document that sets forth your end of life wishes regarding the termination of life-prolonging procedures (respiration, hydration, nutrition) if you are mentally incapacitated and your illness or injury is expected to result in your death.

Personal Representative: Another name for an Executor or Administrator.

Pet Trust: A special trust prepared to ensure your pet receives proper care after you die or in the event you become incapacitated. Contains sufficient funds and instructions to provide lifetime care for your pet. Also names pet caregivers, animal care panel and Trustees.

Pour Over Will: An abbreviated Will used with a Living Trust. It sets forth your instructions regarding guardianship of minor children and the transfer (pour over) of all assets owned in your individual name (probate assets) to your Living Trust.

Power of Attorney: A legal document that gives another person legal authority to act on your behalf for a stated purpose. Ends at revocation, incapacity (unless it is a durable power of attorney) and death.

Probate: The legal process of validating a Will, paying debts, and distributing assets after death. Generally requires the services of a qualified attorney.

Probate Estate: The assets owned in your individual name at death (or assets with beneficiary designations payable to your estate). Does not include assets owned as joint tenants with rights of survivorship, pay-on-death accounts, transfer-on-death designations, insurance payable to a named beneficiary or trust, and other assets with beneficiary designations.

Probate Fees: Legal, Executor/Personal Representative, court, and appraisal fees for an estate that requires probate. Probate fees are paid from assets in the estate before the assets are fully distributed to the heirs.

Revocable Living Trust: Another name for a Living Trust.

Spendthrift Clause: Protects assets in a Trust from a beneficiary's creditors.

Successor Trustee: Person or institution named in a trust document that will take over should the acting Trustee die, resign or otherwise become unable to act.

Tangible Personal Property: Personal property that ordinarily has no registered owner, such as furniture, clothing, jewelry, antiques, collections, etc., but not cash or other financial assets.

Tenancy by the Entirety: A form of joint ownership of property available only to married couples. Very similar to Joint Tenancy in that title to the property automatically vests in the surviving spouse. TBE ownership provides creditor protection in some states.

Tenants in Common: A form of joint ownership whereby a deceased tenant's share passes to his or her heirs or beneficiaries through his or her estate.

Testamentary Trust: A Trust created in a Will or Trust. Only becomes effective at death. May not avoid probate when created in a Will.

Testate: An estate where the decedent died with a valid Will.

Trust Administration: The legal process required to administer trust assets after incapacity or death. Includes the management of trust assets for the named beneficiaries, the payment of debts, taxes or other expenses and the distribution of assets to beneficiaries according to the Trust instructions. Generally requires the services of an attorney.

Trustee: Person, institution or charitable who manages and distributes another's assets according to the instructions in the Trust document.

Will (or Last Will & Testament): A written document with instructions for disposing of assets after death. A Will can only be enforced through the probate court.

Appendix B

ESTATE PLANNING CHECKLIST

Part 1 – Communicating Your Wishes

Do you have a will? A trust?

Are you comfortable with your selection of helpers – attorney in fact, health care surrogates, personal representative/executor or successor trustees?

Have you executed a healthcare power of attorney appointing a healthcare surrogate in the event of catastrophic illness or disability? Are your important family members named as your surrogate for decision making purposes?

Have you memorialized your end-of-life wishes in a living will?

Have you executed a HIPAA authorization that allows your surrogate and other trusted helpers to speak with your health care providers?

Have you executed a durable financial power of attorney for the purpose of appointing an agent (attorney in fact) to handle your financial affairs and property matters, especially in the event of your disability?

Are you comfortable that if you become incapacitated, the local guardianship judge will choose the right person to care for your minor children, or have you have legally chosen those individuals yourself?

Have you named a person or persons as your guardian in the event a guardianship becomes necessary for you?

Have you considered a revocable living trust to consolidate assets, avoid probate, minimize exposure to estate tax and provide long-term protections for your spouse, children, pets and other loved ones?

Does your revocable living trust specify an understandable test to determine your incapacity? Who will participate on your personally selected disability panel?

If you have a living trust, have you titled your assets in the name of the trust? Have you named your trust as the primary beneficiary on your contract assets (i.e., insurance, annuities, and retirement plans)?

Are you comfortable with all of the successor trustees you've selected?

If you have a will, trust or other legal directives, have they been reviewed in the last two years to ensure they are consistent with your wishes, the status of the law and your attorney's changing experience?

Part 2 - Protecting Your Family

Are you comfortable that when you die, the local guardianship judge will choose the right person to raise your minor children and the right person to manage their inheritance (i.e., does your will name a guardian for your minor children)?

Does your estate plan specifically include provisions to protect your spouse, children, pets and other loved ones at the time of your death?

Have you taken steps to protect your children's inheritance in the event your surviving spouse chooses to remarry after your death? Is a prenuptial agreement recommended or required?

Does your plan provide protection for your children and other loved ones from creditors, predators, divorce and, if they need it, from themselves?

Have you recently checked the beneficiary designations of your retirement plans and life insurance policies to ensure you have not listed your estate, your ex-spouse or any minor children as either primary or secondary beneficiaries?

Are you sure you have the right amount and type of life insurance to help with survivor income, loan repayment, capital needs and estate settlement expenses?

Have you considered an irrevocable life insurance trust to exclude the insurance proceeds from being taxed as part of your estate?

Have you considered creating trusts for your spouse, partner or other family to facilitate gift giving?

Part 3 - Helping to Reduce Your Estate and Income Taxes

Do you and your spouse each individually own enough assets to qualify for the applicable exclusion amounts, currently $5.12 million (possible going to $1 million in January 2013)?

If you are unmarried but in a committed relationship, does your estate plan and your partner's take advantage of each of your applicable exclusion amounts while protecting the future distribution of those assets at the death of your partner?

Are you making gifts to your spouse or other family members that maximize the annual gift tax exclusion, currently $13,000?

Have you gifted assets with a strong probability of future appreciation in order to maximize future estate tax savings? Did you use an irrevocable trust?

Have you considered charitable trusts that can provide you with both estate and income tax benefits?

Part 4 - Protecting Your Business

If you own a business, do you have a management succession plan?

Do you have a buy-sell agreement for your business interests?

Do you conduct an annual legal audit of all corporate documents including updated minutes, contracts and insurance policies?

Is your spouse or life partner employed by your business? Have you taken all financial and legal steps necessary to ensure his or her continued participation in the business in the event of your death?

Have you considered a gift program that involves your family-owned business?

Author Biographies

PEGGY R. HOYT, J.D., M.B.A,

Peggy is an attorney, author and entrepreneur who reflects her passion for pets in almost everything she does. She comes by her love of animals naturally as her father was the President and CEO of The Humane Society of the United States from 1970-1997.

Peggy and her law partner, Randy Bryan, own and operate The Law Offices of Hoyt & Bryan, LLC—Family Wealth & Legacy Counsellors, in Oviedo, Florida. Both Peggy and Randy are dual Florida Bar board certified in Wills, Trusts and Estates as well as Elder Law. Their firm limits its practice to estate planning and elder law issues including the creation, maintenance and administration of estate plans that "work." Areas of expertise also include planning for special needs family members, unmarried couples, business succession and of course, pets.

This is Peggy's ninth book. Her first, *All My Children Wear Fur Coats – How to Leave a Legacy for Your Pet,* (**LegacyForYourPet.com**) was inspired by her pets, currently three horses, six dogs (including one service puppy) and four cats. Other co-authored books include *Special People, Special Planning - Creating a Safe Legal Haven for Families with Special Needs; Loving Without a License – An Estate Planning Survival Guide for Unmarried Couples and Same Sex Partners; A Matter of Trust – The Importance of Personal Instructions; Women in Transition – Navigating the Legal and Financial Challenges in Your Life; Like a Library Burning – Saving and Sharing Stories of a Lifetime; Thank Everybody for Everything – Grow Your Life and Business with Gratitude; and Gratitude Expressions – a Five Year Journal.*

In February 2009, Peggy and estate planning colleague Teresa Morgan became SendOutCards Distributors calling themselves the Card Divas. They are currently Senior Managers and use the SendOutCards system both personally and professionally in their daily lives by adopting the philosophy of "making a living through giving."

Peggy is active in a variety of organizations, including WealthCounsel, Central Florida Estate Planning Council and Executive Council member of the General Practice, Solo and Small Firm Section of the Florida Bar. She is a frequent speaker on estate planning and elder law topics, as well as practice management including team training and marketing.

Peggy is married to Joe Allen and spends her "free" time training for limited distance endurance and competitive trail riding events on her Premarin rescue mare, Sierra.

To learn more or to contact Peggy:
PeggyRHoyt@gmail.com
HoytBryan.com
CardDivas.com
PeggyHoyt.com
TheProfessionalNudge.com
AnimalCareTrust.com
PetDisputes.com
CenterForAnimalAdvocacy.com
@PeggyRHoyt
@PetLawyers

DEBORAH E. ROSER, J.D.

Debbie is an attorney, sailor, author and entrepreneur. As owner and operator of Roser Law LLC in Southwest Florida, Debbie provides peace of mind estate planning for her clients. Through a process of education and counseling, Debbie listens carefully to understand each client's unique situation, hopes, dreams, concerns and goals for themselves and their families. Then she works with each client to collaborate on the plan that will work best for their situation and family.

Debbie is married to Craig. Embarking on a grand adventure in 2007, they sold their home and left their work in Connecticut for a two-year sailing hiatus that took them up and down the Eastern Seaboard from Maine to Key West as well as to Bermuda and the Bahamas. As cruisers, they were part of an amazing community of caring, loving and giving individuals, where they made lifetime friendships. Debbie also partnered with friends, Radeen Cochran and Vanessa Williams, to launch an interactive website for women sailors to associate, learn from and help each other. Returning to Florida in 2009, they settled in Southwest Florida, where Debbie joined WealthCounsel and opened her estate planning practice.

Previously, Debbie practiced civil litigation, first in Florida and then as a partner with Litchfield Cavo LLP in Connecticut. Debbie is licensed to practice law in Florida and Connecticut and is a member of WealthCounsel. Debbie is also active in her community. As President Elect of the All Achievers Chapter of the American Business Women's Association, she works to provide scholarships for non-traditional students in her area. She spends her free time playing tennis, reading, writing, and spending time with family and friends.

As business partners, Peggy and Debbie created the publishing company, Gratitude Partners for the purpose of producing books that would enrich a person's life experience. This is their third book. They also founded The Professional Nudge (TheProfessionalNudge.com), a legal letter writing business to assist individuals in resolving disputes without litigation and Animal Care Trust for the purpose of providing trustee services to pet trusts (AnimalCareTrust.com).

Peggy and Debbie both believe we each have the power to create a positive shift in our lives—and those of others—by recognizing our blessings and sharing our gratitude. Together, they wrote *Thank Everybody for Everything! Grow Your Life and Business with Gratitude*, and the co-created *Gratitude Expressions, a Five Year Journal.*

To learn more or to contact Debbie:

Debbie.Roser@gmail.com
RoserLawLLC.com
TheProfessionalNudge.com
AnimalCareTrust.com

www.ingramcontent.com/pod-product-compliance
Lightning Source LLC
Chambersburg PA
CBHW060644210326
41520CB00010B/1732